Read-About® Math

The Shapes We Eat

By Simone T. Ribke

Consultant
Linda Bullock
Reading Consultant

Children's Press®
A Division of Scholastic Inc.
New York   Toronto   London   Auckland   Sydney
Mexico City   New Delhi   Hong Kong
Danbury, Connecticut

Designer: Herman Adler Design
Photo Researcher: Caroline Anderson
The photo on the cover shows different shapes of food.

Library of Congress Cataloging-in-Publication Data

Ribke, Simone T.
  The shapes we eat / by Simone T. Ribke.— 1st ed.
      p. cm. — (Rookie read-about math)
  Includes bibliographical references and index.
  ISBN 0-516-24431-0 (lib. bdg.)   0-516-25848-6 (pbk.)
  1. Geometry—Juvenile literature. 2. Food—Juvenile literature. I. Title. II.
Series.
  QA445.5.R53 2004
  516—dc22

                                    2004005071

What shapes do you eat?

This wheel of cheese
is shaped like a circle. A
circle is round. It has no
sides and no angles. Angles
form where corners meet.

Can you think of other
foods shaped like a circle?

6

This corn chip is shaped like a triangle (TRY-ang-guhl). It has three sides and three angles.

Can you think of other foods shaped like a triangle?

This sandwich is shaped like a square. A square has four sides the same length. It has four angles, too.

Can you think of other foods shaped like a square?

This oat bar is shaped like a rectangle (RECK-tang-guhl). It has four sides. Two are long and two are short. It has four angles, too.

Can you think of other foods shaped like a rectangle?

This egg is shaped like an oval (OH-vuhl). An oval looks like a circle that has been stretched. It has no angles.

Can you think of other foods shaped like an oval?

This slice of cheese is shaped like a pentagon (PEN-tuh-gon). A pentagon has five sides and five angles.

Can you think of other foods shaped like a pentagon?

This cracker is shaped like a hexagon (HEX-uh-gon). A hexagon has six sides and six angles.

Can you think of other foods shaped like a hexagon?

You can put shapes together to make other shapes.

Put two triangles together. Now you have a square. Remember, a square has four sides.

Put two squares together to make a rectangle. Remember, a rectangle has four sides.

Four triangles can also make a rectangle.

Try it!

Together, one square and one triangle can make a pentagon. Remember, a pentagon has five sides.

Six triangles can make a hexagon. Remember, a hexagon has six sides.

Two pentagons can make
an octagon. Remember,
an octagon has eight sides.

What other shapes can you
make with food?

The foods we eat come in many different shapes. There are round grapes, square sandwiches, and oval eggs.

What shapes do you eat?

Words You Know

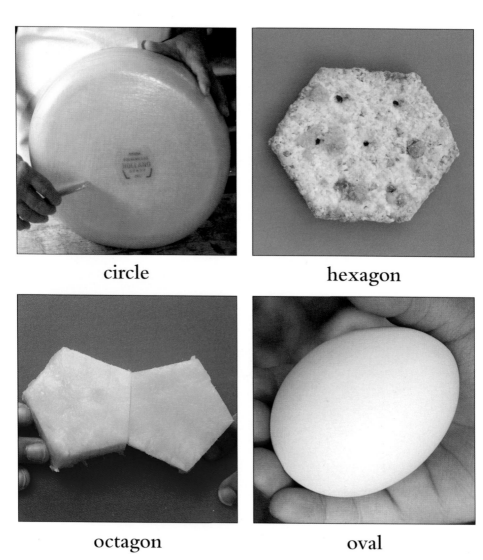

circle

hexagon

octagon

oval